Jackson W. Carroll

Ministry as Reflective Practice:

a new look at the professional model

an Alban Institute Publication

Jackson W. Carroll is Professor of Religion in Society and Director of Research at Hartford Seminary. He is an ordained United Methodist minister and has served as both parish and campus minister. He is author of numerous books and articles on American church life, with a particular focus on congregations and clergy. Two recently co-authored books include *Women of the Cloth* and *Varieties of Religious Presence*. He is also co-editor of the *Handbook for Congregational Studies*.

The Publications Program of The Alban Institute is assisted by a grant from Trinity Church, New York City.

Introduction: A Model of Ministry Under Critique

There is considerable confusion presently about authority in the church—that of the ordained clergy, of the laity in relation to clergy, and of the church more generally as it attempts to carry out its mission in society. The first two of these confusions partly derive from what the title of an Alban Institute publication called *The Mystery of Clergy Authority*[1] and partly, I believe, to muddled thinking about ministry in the church and the respective roles of clergy professionals and laity. Confusion centers especially in what has come to be called "the professional model of ministry." My purpose here is to examine this model of ministry, which has been dominant in recent years, and its relationship to authority in the church. Given the criticisms, which will be examined in some detail, one might ask the question: Is the professional model worth saving? I believe that the answer to this question is affirmative; however, the model is badly in need of rethinking in its application to ministry. Thus I also attempt to suggest some ways in which I believe it needs to be reconceived rather than "scrapped" as some of its critics maintain.[2]

Let me begin with a brief note about authority, although the broader topic of clergy authority is beyond my concern here. By authority I mean legitimate power. To exercise authority is to influence, direct, coordinate or otherwise guide the thought and behavior of persons and groups in ways that are considered legitimate by those persons and/or groups. The minister's authority is principally what some have called *cultural* authority as distinct from *social* authority. The former has to do with the right to control or influence another's definitions of reality and judgments of meaning and value, while social authority has to do with the right to control or influence another's behavior. In an ultimate sense, it can be said that all authority in the church derives (or ought to derive) from God; however, we can think also of penultimate or secondary bases of authority in the church. Elsewhere in a discussion of clergy authority[3], I outlined two penultimate bases of authority exercised by clergy: authority derived from the clergyperson's special relationship to God, and authority derived from one's expertise, including knowledge and skills important for the religious community and its members. I further characterized each of these two bases of authority by whether it is predominantly grounded in the minister's personal attributes and/or sanctity or in her or his entry through ordination into the formal office of priest or ordained minister.

perhaps add auth. der. from rel. w people?

These distinctions have implications for our models of ministry. When a special relationship to God has been the primary basis of the minister's authority, the ensuing models of ministry have emphasized more the ordained minister as representative of God, either by virtue of personal spirituality/charisma or of an office in which charisma has been institutionalized—for example, the priesthood. When expertise has been the primary basis of the ordained minister's authority, the emphasis has been more on the minister as professional, whether as preacher, teacher, pastor, or parish manager. Like one's relationship to God, such expertise may also be a quality of the person, whether officially recognized or not, or an attribute ascribed to the institutional role of professional clergy and officially recognized in ordination.

In reality these distinctions rarely exist in pure form. The models by which persons operate in ordained ministry are typically a combination of the emphases. Relationship to God and expertise are not mutually exclusive, as we shall see, and the same is true for personal and institutional sources of authority. Nevertheless, we can, in fact, speak of an *evangelical* model of ordained ministry that emphasizes the personal piety of the clergyperson above all else—as evident in the considerable concern in an earlier period of our nation's history for a "converted ministry." And we can speak also of a *priestly* or *sacramental* model of ordained ministry that places primary emphasis on the sacramental role of the person who mediates between God and humankind by virtue of her or his institutional office. Likewise, too, we can speak of a *professional* model of ordained ministry that places heavy emphasis on the expertise—both knowledge and skills—of the clergyperson and its application in the life of the church.

It is this latter model that is our particular concern. Being granted authority as a professional to provide important and valued services in a particular area of human life has come to be sought after by various occupational groups in contemporary society, in part because of the rewards—social and psychic as well as monetary—that are granted to professionals. Additionally, being viewed as a professional has signaled, correctly or not, a standard of excellence in specialized knowledge and skills.

It is not surprising, therefore, that the ordained ministry has also come to be thought of as a profession, and that there has been considerable discussion about its character as a profession, its place among modern professions, and how theological schools and continuing education opportunities can be improved to enable clergy to become more professional. A variety of studies of the ordained ministry have used the professional model as a framework for analysis as well as for comparison of clergy with other professions. Sometimes also the concept of a profession has been used as a kind of rallying call for clergy, demoralized by questions about the viability of the church in modern, secular society and their role in it, to take themselves and their status seriously as an ancient and honored occupation. While James Glasse's book *Profession Minister*[4] had a broader agenda than this, such a concern seems clearly to have been part of its intent, as its subtitle, "Confronting the Identity Crisis of the Parish Clergy," makes clear. In theological education, concern with ministry as a profession has involved a call to seminaries and continuing theological educators to enable clergy to take seriously the practice of ministry in such a way that what ministers actually do forms the core of the curriculum. Indeed the professional model of ministry has been the dominant emphasis of the Association of Theological Schools in its accrediting and programmatic emphases at least since the early 1960s. The development of the Doctor of Ministry degree as a professional doctorate has been one of the major fruits of this emphasis. Finally, too, one might also note the dominance of the professional model in the development of clinical pastoral education and in pastoral counseling as a specialized form of the profession of ministry.

In recent years, however, an increasing stream of criticism has been directed at the professional model in general and the professional model of ordained ministry in particular. It has been faulted variously for:

- perpetuating a notion of the need for distinctive expertise and rigorous education for an occupation that no longer requires it, if it ever did;
- making it impossible, if not difficult, to meet the needs of churches which cannot afford, or perhaps do not even require, full-time ordained leadership;
- creating a dependent laity and subverting the ministry of the whole people of God;
- ignoring the distinctive theological and/or sacramental dimensions of ministry while concentrating on functional competence;
- fragmenting the theological curriculum by making the various ministerial roles, rather than theological understanding, the primary focus of theological education;
- ignoring or de-emphasizing calling to the ministry.

These various criticisms of the professional model of ministry are, I believe, related to the confusion that exists about authority for ministry, both ordained and lay. Thus, to repeat, it is my purpose here to examine several of the more important of these criticisms, to assess their validity, and to propose a way of thinking about ordained ministry as a profession that avoids some of the more serious problems that critics of the professional model have raised. For all the problems entailed in conceiving ordained ministry as a profession, I simply do not believe that the church can afford to have ordained leadership unable to function with the kind of competence that we have come to associate with the word professional.

What is the Professional Model?

In order to examine the various criticisms of the professional model of ministry, it is necessary first to indicate what is typically meant by the term. Here the "rub" begins, because, as will become evident, there is no single understanding of the professional model of ministry common to all of the critiques. Each often focuses on one or another aspect of the model. Let me therefore take a brief and considerably oversimplified look at the history of the concept of a profession, especially as it applies to ordained ministry, as a means of sharpening our understanding of the criticisms of the professional model of ministry.

The concept of "profession" is an ancient one, having its western roots in the Judeo-Christian tradition and especially in the religious orders of the medieval Christian church. To be professed in vows, as John Westerhoff has written, "was to have acknowledged a special grace related to an intimate, relational knowledge of God (faith), given by God (revelation) and calling one to a corresponding responsibility to live for the good of others (vocation), through some particular form of service (ministry)."[6] A person was called to profess publicly his or her faith and vocation and to enter a community through whose aid he or she would give expression to this faith and vocation. The monasteries provided such communities; and because there was no separation of the sacred and profane, the monasteries became centers of service, culture and learning where those who were professed were concerned not only with scripture and theology, but philosophy and science, medicine and law.

As universities developed and as society became more complex and less under the domination of the church, separate professions developed—medicine, law, architecture, ministry—and lost their specific association with the priesthood. Though moving toward the modern meaning of profession, these early professions were still some distance from what we mean today when we use the term. Rather, a pre-nineteenth century professional, clergy included, tended to be primarily a learned gentleman, a person with a liberal education supplemented by practical skills typically learned on the job, often under the tutelage of a senior member of the profession. To be a professional was as much, if not more, a status to which one belonged by virtue of one's culture and education in a hierarchically ordered society as it was a specific occupation in which one engaged, or a self-conscious occupational group to which one belonged. Indeed, many pre-nineteenth century professionals—doctors, lawyers and clergy—were not especially learned, and it perhaps stretches the point to refer to them as professionals, except in terms of the status they occupied in the community. Nor were their roles as separate and specialized as they later became. As Anthony Russell has shown in his analysis of clergy in the Church of England, many parsons continued to perform multiple roles in rural England as administrators of the Poor Law, political agents, teachers, registrars, medical practitioners, policemen and even sanitary engineers.[7]

Beginning in the early to mid-nineteenth century, as both Great Britain and America were changing from essentially rural and agrarian to urban and industrial societies, the older "status" professions were transformed and, along with emerging new professions, became more specifically occupationally defined and organized to meet the specialized needs for knowledge and services in the new type of society. In each society, a large middle class emerged with the older and newer professionals as a leading element. In his important history of the rise of modern professions, Burton Bledstein writes that "The most emphatically middle class man was the professional, improving his worldly lot as he offered his special knowledge and services to society, expressing his expanding expectations as ascending stages of an occupation."[8] Each old and new profession sought the right to develop and control educational requirements and licensing of practitioners, leading to many "turf" conflicts within and between professions[9].

Also of great significance at this time was the rise of modern science and technology. It became important to the emerging professions to demonstrate that their practice was grounded in a scientifically based theory that could be translated into skills for addressing important human problems. Improving and/or developing schools for the education of the new professionals provided a major impetus in the large scale growth of universities and university-related professional schools in the late nineteenth century, especially in the United States. Such schools were crucial for qualifying and certifying persons as fit for professional practice.

These changes had a considerable impact on professions in general and the ministry in particular. Writing of New England Congregational ministers, Donald Scott, in his book, *From Office to Profession*,[10] contrasts their earlier position as essentially local officials within a well-defined and ordered theocentric communalism with that which developed by the mid-nineteenth century:

> ...by the 1850s, in institutional terms, the clergy had become a profession, a coherent, self-conscious occupational body, organized and defined by a set of institutions which were outside lay or public control, which controlled the special learning needed to become a clergyman, and which possessed the power to determine who could enter the clerical ranks.... Whether a pastor or not, the clergyman's essential orientation...,was now toward the profession. It created him, sustained his sense of himself as a clergyman, defined his role and provided the most important community of which he felt himself a part and by which he distinguished himself from other groups in the society. In addition, it was as a "professional" that one gained the standing to represent organized Christianity and convey it to whatever constituencies one might serve. Moreover, its character as a profession enhanced the clergy's collective legitimacy as the overall guardian and definer of God's word and presence in society. Under the culture of professionalism, monopoly properly belonged to the collective body of certified practitioners, those who had gone through the rituals and training (which only those already through them could define and control) that made one a "professional" rather than a layman or amateur.

Under the leadership of educators such as William Rainey Harper, President of the University of Chicago, there were concurrent efforts to reform the education of ministers along more professional lines, especially seeking a scientific basis for practice and placing a heavy emphasis on skills needed in that practice. The development of biblical criticism, efforts to develop a scientific theology, and especially the virtual "explosion" in the field of practical theology were among the most important late nineteenth and early twentieth century efforts to foster a scientific approach in theological education.

Thus, the recent emphasis on the professional model of ministry in Protestant theological education, and increasingly among Roman Catholics as well, is the fruition of the development of this modern understanding of a profession, though continuities with its more ancient roots have not been lost. Reflecting the modern understanding in particular, and also the more general approval of the professional model, Professor George F. Moore of Harvard wrote in the *Hartford Seminary Record* of 1908:

> The ministry is a (practical) calling like law and medicine, and preparation for it should be directed, unified, and limited by the practical end. Just as it is not the primary end of the law school to produce men learned in the history and philosophy of jurisprudence, but to train

men to (practice) law in their own country and time; as it is not the primary end of the medical school to make men learned in the history and theory of medicine, but to train physicians to practice the healing art in their own generation; so it is not the primary end of the theological school to send out men learned in the history and philosophy of religion, but to train men for the practice of ministry.[11]

Moore's plea found strong advocates in various studies of theological education earlier in the twentieth century which called for reforms of the educational process to emphasize what ministers actually do.

It is these developments, along with the importance attributed to the professional model generally in our society, that must be taken into account as one attempts to understand the recent emphasis on ordained ministry as a profession as well as the criticisms. To be sure, important continuities exist with the older heritage of the professions, but I believe that these more recent developments often obscure some of the continuities.

What then are the critical elements of the professional model? Let me cite the definition of a profession used by sociologist Wilbert Moore in a recent book on the professions.[12] Moore's list of professional attributes is not only a useful summary of what are generally considered basic characteristics of a profession, but in his list it is possible to see some traces of the pre-modern view of a professional as well as the more modern emphases. Moore views a profession as: (1) a *full- time* occupation, which sets the professional off from the amateur; (2) having a sense of *calling*, that is, the treatment of the occupation and all of its requirements as an enduring set of normative and behavioral expectations; (3) being *set apart from the laity* by various signs and symbols, while at the same time identifying with one's peers, often in a formalized organization; (4) possessing esoteric but useful *knowledge and skills* based on specialized training of exceptional duration and perhaps of exceptional difficulty; (5) having a *service orientation* which puts the needs of the client(s) above self-interest; and (6) thus enjoying *autonomy* restrained by responsibility in the exercise of one's knowledge and skills. Moore emphasizes that each of the criteria should be considered as a variable which a given profession may meet more or less, thus allowing for comparison of various occupations on a scale of professionalization. That, however, is not my intent; instead, I find his categories helpful as a capsule summary of what is implied by the professional model as well as a point of reference for examining the various criticisms of the professional model as applied to the ordained ministry.

Criticisms of the Professional Model

With this historical and conceptual background now sketched in, I return to the criticisms of the professional model of ministry. As noted, there are a number of different points at which the model has been criticized. I will not try to deal with them all, but only with three which seem to me to be particularly important. Let me illustrate them by giving three scenarios.

1. A pastor believes strongly that ministry is to be shared between clergy and laity. Yet she is constantly frustrated by what I call the "I'm just a layperson" syndrome; that is, by having laity in the congregation defer to her expertise in all matters. They say to her: "We don't know enough about the Bible or theology to teach an adult church school class. We want you to to do it." "We have a hard time seeing the connection between our beliefs and what we do at work, or how our faith relates to political issues. We're just laity. You tell us. You're the professional. You're the authority when it comes to the church and ministry. We're amateurs."

2. In another congregation, the laity are relatively satisfied with the skills of their pastor. He's a "pro" when it comes to leading groups. He's up-to-date on the latest theories and techniques of management, group dynamics and organizational development. While his skills in other ministry roles are not quite so good, he is at least adequate in these areas and attends workshops to improve his skills. But all is not well. Members sense a deficiency which is hard for them to define but is nevertheless real in their experience. When it comes to helping members to develop a vision for their church's ministry and mission, or helping them to understand the relationship of the Gospel to issues and crises that arise in the course of their lives, their pastor is not much help. In short, they find his leadership within the congregation to be rather shallow and limited.

3. In yet another congregation, there is a pastor who is also acknowledged as competent. Not only does he have adequate managerial and group leadership skills, but he has other strengths as well. His sermons are usually well-prepared; he seems to have a good knowledge of the Bible and theology; he knows how to counsel those who come to him with problems; and, unlike the pastor in the second scenario, he is able to articulate a theological vision for the congregation and help people think theologically about their lives. But the laity of the congregation are also aware that something is missing. As best as they can describe it, their pastor lacks spiritual depth. His ministry exhibits more "head than heart." For all his knowledge and skills, there is a lack of authenticity and even integrity for which his considerable knowledge and skills are not an adequate compensation.

Each of these scenarios illustrates one of the reasons why the professional model of ministry has come under fire in recent years. It creates a dependent laity and denies, therefore, the ministry of the whole people of God. Or, it focuses education for ministry—both M.Div. and continuing education—on learning a number of discrete theories and skills, but it fails to to help ministers to learn to think theologically and bring their theological insights to bear in any coherent way on the issues of ministry practice. And, finally, the model emphasizes expertise and skills to the point of neglecting the calling of ministers and their spiritual authenticity. Let us examine each of these criticism briefly.

(1) Creating a Dependent Laity

First, there is the criticism that the professional model creates a dependent laity by holding up the clergy as experts who have a monopoly over important aspects of the church's life. Along with this is the tendency for the professional model simply to set clergy and laity off from one another and create separate "classes" of Christians.

The latter situation is not the fault alone of the professional model, but goes back at least to the fourth century when a hierarchical understanding of the ministry developed under neoplatonic influences. As Bernard Cooke[13] has expressed it:

> What this means among other things is that the clergy became increasingly a separate class in Christian society; they were not "ordinary people." They were above the laity not just in the dignity of their functions within the community but in the very nature of their membership in the church.

Anti-clericalism, which has a long history, is in part a reaction against this kind of hierarchical understanding of ministry. While the United States has been relatively free of the extreme anti-clericalism that has afflicted a number of European and Latin American nations, the several Awakenings in American Protestantism have typically been followed by conflicts between clergy and revitalized laity who have wished to claim the validity of their own ministry. Thus, conflicts and tensions over who does ministry have a much longer history than the professional model.

However, the modern notion of professionalism in the ordained ministry has also contributed to the problem, especially when coupled with the anti-hierarchy, pro-participatory democracy ethos characteristic of American society since the counter cultural revolution of the late 1960s. The specialized training of the professional clergyperson does give her or him expertise relevant for the church's ministry that the laity do not have. Quite apart from whether the clergyperson chooses to "flaunt" this difference, simply having the expertise inevitably sets her or him apart from the laity to an extent and thereby fosters some dependence on the laity's part. It is a part of the minister's authority.

When to this situation is added the restriction of administration of the sacraments to the ordained role (which is not limited to the professional model), there is a division which lends itself to creation of status differences within the congregation. Whether intended or not, laity come often to view themselves as amateurs in ministry—and may also be viewed as such by clergy. As a consequence, if a layperson becomes really serious about the faith, he or she is frequently encouraged to "go into the ministry"—that is, prepare for ordination—under the tacit or explicit assumption that only then is one really in ministry. Several years ago, when I was involved in a study of the job market for clergy, I interviewed a number of seminarians about their reasons for seeking ordination. I was surprised by the considerable number—especially older seminarians—who indicated that their primary reason for wanting to be ordained grew out of a sense of the spiritual deficiency of the lay status. *Real* ministry is ordained ministry, was the message they communicated.[14]

Even the setting where the professional education for ministry takes place—the seminary (with the original meaning of a "seed plot protected from the world")—has a distancing effect for clergy and laity. The educational experience is removed from where ministry occurs in and through the congregation and in the world. The founding of Andover in 1808 as the first Protestant seminary in the United States created, as Donald Scott notes, "a separate, exclusively ministerial institution. . . [which] in effect removed the clerical candidate from earlier forms of immersion in broader secular institutions and communities."[15] This, in turn, fostered a consciousness in the candidate of being a "professional" as distinct from a layperson.

Additionally, the professional model emphasizes the identification of professional clergy with their clergy peers, often within a formal organization. The organization for the clergy is typically the denomination, or the ministerial "brotherhood" (now to be expanded to include "sisters" as well). In his analysis of the change from the practice of a permanently settled clergy in New England, where clergy typically stayed in one parish throughout their ministry, to one of a ministerial career with successive positions through which one moves, historian Daniel Calhoun has shown how the denomination and ministerial associations assumed increased saliency as a point of identification for the clergy. He cites a blatant example of clerical professional*ism* in an address by Edwards A. Park of Andover Seminary to the Pastoral Association of the Congregational Ministers in Massachusetts in 1844. Park "wanted the clergy to accept professionalism and the mass society through a single strategy: let ministers accept the fact that they were an order set apart from the laity, an order whose competent concern for theology they could not communicate to the mass; let them derive their standing and their prestige from each other, 'dispensing a popular product to the populace and reserving abstruse theological discussion for their private meetings.'"[16]

For these various reasons, one must admit that among the liabilities of the professional model is its tendency to foster a sense of the professional as set apart from the laity, just as it also can encourage creation of a dependent laity. This has led some critics to question the need for any form of professionally trained parish clergy and to propose alternatives such as that, for example, espoused by the Theological Education by Extension Movement. The movement advocates raising up indigenous leadership in each local congregation and providing the necessary training through various models of extension education. Such a model, it is believed, enlivens the shared ministry of the whole people of God in ways not possible when there is a professionally trained clergy.

(2) A Non-theological Approach to Ministry

The second scenario—the pastor whose considerable skills are devoid of a unifying vision for ministry—reflects concern about the nature of the core expertise necessary for ministry, especially what is the relation of theology to the practice of ministry. Critics believe that the wedding of theological education, including continuing theological education, to the professional model of ministry has led to an emphasis on learning particular bodies of knowledge—for example, Bible, theology, church history—and particular skills of ministry—for example, preaching, counseling, administration; however, *there is little or nothing that gives coherence to these discrete bodies of knowledge and skills.* There is no theological core which enables a person to integrate the various elements, to bring together theology and practice into an integrated whole. Instead, theology has become itself a separate discipline among others. The problem is reflected in the organization of the typical seminary curriculum with its division into discrete fields of study.[17] And the result of this fragmentation is frequently a non-reflective and non-theological approach to ministry that is illustrated by the second scenario.

The pastor in the scenario is an example of what the philosopher Alasdair MacIntyre has described as a problem that affects all professions in modern society. There is an assumption that questions about ultimate values and goals cannot be settled rationally. Rationality is primarily utilitarian or instrumental; and acting rationally means choosing means that are believed to be useful and effective in achieving one's ends. Whether one's ends or purposes are good or true in any ultimate sense is beyond the capacity of reason to judge; so typically, those ends go unexamined. As a result, says MacIntyre, dominant professional models of our day reflect either the *Manager* or the *Therapist*. The former applies the techniques of organizational science to enable their organizations to achieve their purposes, which are generally accepted without question. The latter adopts a similar approach to individuals, applying therapeutic techniques to help them clarify their values or goals or find self-realization, but the validity or morality of their values or goals is not questioned.[18]

The pastor who adopts either the Managerial or Therapist model is the one who somewhat uncritically and mechanically adopts the latest version of "twelve steps to effective ministry" or other fad or innovation which promises church growth or better youth programs without a careful analysis of her or his situation, and, more importantly, without asking what vision of ministry or Christian existence is implied in the theories and techniques. We have done the same with psychological or sociological theories. The considerable enthusiasm with which we embraced Freudian, Jungian or Transactional analysis, Human Potential therapies, various theories and skills of organizational development, or Marxist categories, without putting their assumptions to a theological critique, are examples. If one needs any corroboration of this tendency to ride uncritically the latest managerial or therapeutic fads, one has only to look at the range of topics for continuing education events in the advertisements that cross a clergyperson's desk in a typical year. Presumably there is a market for such events. It is not that such skills and theories are necessarily inappropriate. In fact, they are often quite helpful and important; however, the problem comes when they are uncritically appropriated, when they exhibit what MacIntyre calls instrumental reason and do not reflect a critically developed theology and vision of ministry. Divorced from such a vision of the purpose of the church, such skills and theories could be used, with great competence, to build up the church as a unit of the Ku Klux Klan, to put the problem as sharply as possible. And that, say some critics, is at the heart of the problem of the professional model of ministry with its heavy emphasis on functions of ministry in the absence of a critically thought out theological vision that gives coherence to the functions.

(3) Doing Rather Than Being

The third scenario—the minister who has the skills but lacks spiritual depth—focuses on a related yet different criticism of the professional model. With its heavy emphasis on acquiring the knowledge and skills necessary for competent ministry, the professional model of ministry neglects the calling of ministers and the formation of their spiritual life. The result is often competent pastors, like the one in the scenario, who lack the spiritual authenticity and integrity that have been associated with both the sacramental and evangelical models of ministry, where, as I noted earlier (see above, page 2), the minister's relationship to God has priority.

From the Catholic tradition in which the sacramental or priestly role of the ordained person is central, the critique focuses on the tendency of the professional model to emphasize what a person does rather that what she or he is. *Doing* is emphasized over *being*. Thus, professional education focuses more heavily on knowledge and skills for ministry than on the spiritual formation of the priest, on developing and nurturing that kind of spiritual depth, insight and authenticity that enables the priest to represent God before his or her people and the people before God. The late Urban Holmes was one who sharply criticized the professional model of ministry for its neglect of the non-rational and transcendent qualities that make the priest a "sacramental person" or "mystagogue." "To be a mystagogue," says Holmes, "is to lead people into the mystery that surrounds our life. . . deepening humanity's understanding of itself by word and action, by the very nature of the priest's presence."[19] That task he sees as being in sharp contrast to the instrumental roles of ministry emphasized in modern professionalism.

The evangelical Protestant analogue to this critique centers in the concern that the professional model ignores or minimizes the importance of God's call to persons to the ministry. God's call to ministry is an "event," a gift of the spirit which is not taken seriously or even seen as necessary by those who stress the professional model with its emphasis on knowledge and skills.

Neither version of this critique of the professional model is new. Shamed by the moral laxity of the clergy, the Council of Trent in the sixteenth century established seminaries, which as was noted previously, literally meant "seed plots" protected from the world. The seminaries in this model functioned to provide an intensive experience, sheltered from the world, in which the spirituality of candidates for the priesthood could be nurtured and formed. Academic concerns and pastoral skills were secondary; religious formation was primary.

Among Protestants, a similar concern for "an unconverted ministry" was expressed in the struggle between the "Log College" men, led by Gilbert Tennent, and the anti-revivalists among the Philadelphia Presbytery in the 18th century. The issue at this time focused on the tension between the inward call of God in the conversion experience and the outward call from the church in ordination. Was the former necessarily prior to the latter? This was not at all an academic question. There was considerable acceptance of the view that ministerial training was a generally sufficient guarantee of a candidate's worthiness to enter the ordained ministry. The sense of a call may come gradually later, if it came at all. Gilbert Tennent's very definite response to this situation was expressed in his classic sermon, "The Danger of an Unconverted Ministry," where, among other things, he compared an unconverted minister with "a Man who would learn others to swim before he had learn'd it himself, and so is drowned in the Act, and dies like a fool. . . ."[20] By the mid-nineteenth century, Robert Baird could claim that, among evangelical Christians, the matter which concerned Tennent so deeply had been settled. Wrote Baird: ". . . all [evangelical Christians] agree as to the necessity of having a truly regenerated ministry. . . . A regenerated and devoted ministry must be the first of all earthly blessings to a Church, and it is the only instrument that can effectually secure the morals of a community, and the stability of a government."[21] Many contemporary critics of the professional model maintain that the issue has once more become "unsettled."

These then are some of the problems at issue in the professional model as applied to ordained ministry. In light of these and other liabilities, we might ask again: Is it worth saving? As I said earlier, I happen to believe that it is worth saving, but that it very badly needs rethinking in ways that make it more appropriate for ministry. I believe that it is important to undertake this reconceptualization, not out of any sentimental attachment to the professional model or because of a hope that thinking of the ministry as a profession enhances its occupational status, but because I believe that there are significant strengths and emphases in the professional model that should not be lost amidst the criticisms. Indeed, whether we continue to refer to ordained ministry as a profession is ultimately of little consequence, though I suspect that we will continue to do so given the widespread acceptance of the professional model generally as a way of delivering important services. However, if we are to continue to refer to the professional model of *ministry*, then we need to do so in ways appropriate to the church; and that is the focus of my final sections.

Rethinking the Professional Model of Ministry: The Reflective Practitioner

In rethinking the professional model of ministry, I believe that the starting point must be with ecclesiology, that is, with an understanding of the church. I am increasingly convinced that many of our concerns about ministry—especially ordained ministry and the professional model—arise from our tendency to think about ministry in isolation from basic convictions about the church. It is impossible here to attempt adequate consideration of the assumptions about the church which I believe are necessary for rethinking the professional model of ministry; however, I will attempt simply and briefly to state several and then relate them to needed revisions in the professional model.[22] What then are the assumptions that I make about the church?

1. First, I believe that the church is a community which provides, through its gathered life, a context in which persons are enabled to understand their lives and experiences in light of God's self-revelation in history, preeminently in the history of Jesus Christ. In this sense, it is a community of meaning. It is also a community of belonging, where individuals are called out of their loneliness and isolation into caring, supportive relationships with others who share a commitment to Jesus Christ and where they are nurtured in the virtues of Christian life—the fruits of the Spirit of which Paul writes in Galatians. But the community of meaning and belonging which characterizes the gathered life of the church is not an end in itself but a means for the empowerment of members, corporately and individually, to use their gifts in the continuing ministry of Jesus in the world. It is a ministry committed to the cause of God which is the fulfillment of the kingdom of peace and justice among humankind and in the whole of creation. And in both its gathered and scattered life, the church as community is called to be a present sign and foretaste of that kingdom.

2. Second, I believe that the ministry of the church is the task of the whole people of God, clergy and lay. Every Christian is called, by virtue of a common baptism, to use his or her distinctive gifts for the service of God in the world. Any adequate understanding of ministry, professional or otherwise, must take this shared ministry into account.

3. Third, I believe that sharing the ministry does not imply a sameness of functions for all Christians. There is a clear need for a differentiation of functions that has been present in the Christian community from the beginning. While St. Paul's metaphor of the Body of Christ in I Corinthians 12 may not refer specifically to lay-clergy relationships in the modern sense, it clearly recognizes the need for a differentiation of functions within the Body for its own health. The growth of the church in size and complexity since St. Paul's time has increased the need for such differentiation on functional lines. This was, I believe, the major reason for the development of a set-apart ministry in the church as it developed in the post-apostolic period. It became necessary on functional grounds to set apart those with gifts of leadership and the competence to exercise those gifts for the health of the church. Although this does not necessarily imply a professional ministry in the modern sense of the term, neither does it exclude it.

4. Finally, I believe that the primary ministries of laypersons are not in the gathered life of the church but in its scattered life. To be sure, laity share in aspects of the leadership of the gathered life of the church and have gifts for ministry that they are called to exercise there; however, it is in primarily in their daily lives—at work, in the community, at home, in the various public spheres—that they are called to Christian praxis. And, while the ministry of the professional clergy is not restricted to the gathered life of the church, it is that sphere that has priority for them.

Now these assumptions about the church and its ministry are hardly novel; however, they provide the framework into which a reconceptualization of the professional model of ministry needs to be fit. Let me simply note that most of my focus is on the ordained minister as professional. If I seem to slight lay ministry in the process, I do so only because my major concern here is with ordained leadership, not because I do not take lay ministry with equal seriousness.[23]

(1) The Professional Minister and the Laity

On the basis of these assumptions about the church, I begin with the first criticism: the relationship of the ordained professional minister and the laity. As I indicated above, the problem is not wholly that of the professional model. Clericalism has been with us in the church much longer than the professional model of ministry; however, there is no doubt that the model has contributed in its own way to the problem and that we need to be clear about what is different about professional leadership in the church and the situation of other professions.

This involves recognizing first of all that the typical ordained minister who is pastor of a parish has already departed from the general model of the professional which has emphasized the individual professional in a one-to-one relationship with a single client or patient. Instead, she or he relates to a congregation. And, although the congregation is made up of individuals whom the pastor often engages on a one-to-one basis as a professional, the congregation's functioning qua congregation—as an organized entity—is a part of the responsibility of the pastor and requires a particular set of competencies about which I will say more later.

Furthermore, to continue the contrast with the traditional professional model, the members of the congregation are not clients or patients, but are themselves called to exercise ministries among each other and in the particular situations in which they find themselves in everyday life. This is different from the physician's patient, in the traditional medical model, who is not expected to engage in medical practice, or the lawyer's client, who is not expected to practice law. But as my assumptions about shared ministry make clear, laity are expected to join with the professional minister in the ministry of the church. Thus there is the expectation of collegiality with lay members built into the practice of the clergy professional that is not present in the traditional model of the professional as one set apart from the laity.

It is worth noting that in both medicine and law there are strong advocates for a shift away from keeping patients and clients in a dependent relationship. In medicine, for example, the concern is to shift from a "sickness" to a "wellness" orientation, practicing preventive medicine rather than focusing only on illness. The physician's primary role becomes an enabler of health, helping individuals and communities to take greater responsibility for their own physical wellbeing, rather than one solely of treating dependent patients who are ill. Such an approach can have a transformative approach on medical practice as George W. Webber has pointed out.[24] Citing the experience of Cuba, where physicians are paid the same salary regardless of the number of patients they see, he notes that Cuban physicians work hard at preventive medicine. That way they have less work to do. There is a lesson here for clergy. Clergy who are willing to share ministry with laity may or may not have less work to do; however, their work will be different from that of the "super pastors" who anxiously assume that all responsibility for ministry belongs to them and thus keep laity in a dependent role.

But, if my third and fourth assumptions about the need for a differentiation of functions and different primary spheres of ministry are correct, then there are differences of gifts and differences of roles for the various members of the body which require differing competencies for their exercise. In work with both groups, I often find that considerable confusion exists over these differences: laity are sometimes hesitant to claim any gift for ministry or to identify what they do in their daily lives as ministry; clergy often ask, "If all share in ministry, then what is distinctive about my role as an ordained minister?" Clergy and laity need help in understanding the differences of functions and in developing the expertise needed for these differentiated functions, while not losing sight of the collegial ministry in which all share.

Continuing my focus primarily on the clergy role, let me elaborate briefly on several areas in which distinctive clergy leadership is especially needed. In doing so, I must add that few clergy will be equally gifted in all three areas that I discuss; however, if they are to provide the leadership needed in the congregation, they will need to have some expertise in each area.

In my first assumption about the church (see above, page 15), I described three tasks of the church. As it participates in the continuing ministry of Jesus, it functions as a community of meaning, belonging, and empowerment. These three areas are useful in describing particular areas in which clergy leadership is needed: as meaning definers or interpreters, as community builders, and, for lack of a better term, as managers of the interface between the church and its social context.

As definer or interpreter of meaning, especially through the roles of preacher, liturgist-celebrant, teacher, and counselor, the ordained minister has the task of assisting other members of the church to reflect on and interpret their personal and social experiences—hopes, fears, disappointments, moral dilemmas and life crises—in light of God's purposes in Jesus Christ. Such a task requires a kind of reflective expertise that I will describe in more detail below: the capacity to draw on one's knowledge and personal experience in an effort to analyze and understand particular issues or situations; the capacity to interpret the issues or situations in light of the Christian story in an informed and persuasive manner; and a willingness to honor and learn from the insights and experiences of the others (or other) in the situation.

Let me illustrate what I mean in one area of life. Recently, as a part of a research project on the role of religion in public life we interviewed in some depth a variety of Hartford, Connecticut, civic leaders. Many of them, who are also active lay members of congregations, emphasized the importance they attached to moral reflection on public as well as personal issues and their desire to be involved in such reflection in their congregations. Though they looked to clergy to facilitate such reflection, a number expressed disappointment because of the failure of their pastors to do so. When pushed to say more precisely what they desired from clergy, the leaders emphasized that they were not looking for prescriptions or pronouncements regarding the issues; rather, they wanted clergy who were willing to join with them in trying to understand the issues at hand, who were willing and able to bring their expertise as interpreters of a religious tradition to bear on the issues, and who were willing be partners with them in reflecting on the theological and moral dimensions of the issues.[25] James Gustafson refers to this particular interpretative role of the clergy as that of "moral counselor."[26] The kind of careful analyses and interpretations that the Roman Catholic bishops have recently brought to issues of nuclear arms and capitalism are special instances of the kind of moral counseling that is called for from "rank and file" clergy in less dramatic and often more ordinary issues in their meaning defining or interpretive roles in preaching, teaching and pastoral counseling. Parishioners also look for help not only with issues of social or public ethics but with personal morality, marriage and family crises, teaching their children about issues of faith and morals, and facing suffering and death—their own and that of loved ones.

The church is also a community of belonging in which, I suggested, individuals are called out of their loneliness and isolation into caring, supportive relationships with others who share a commitment to Jesus Christ, and where they are nurtured in the virtues of Christian life. Here, too, leadership is needed in building or facilitating such community. This involves both theological insight into the nature of Christian community and its purpose in the world and skills in assisting such community to happen in and through the church: managerial and administrative skills, skills in group relationships and conflict management, and political and persuasive skills. There is also a close relationship between the clergy's role as celebrant of the sacraments and building up the community—for example, bringing people together around the table in the eucharist, or celebrating the incorporation of individuals into the family of God in baptism. In these various roles, the aim is building up and edifying the community and enabling its members to grow into maturity as Christians.

In his book, *The Purpose of the Church and Its Ministry*, H. Richard Niebuhr used the image of "pastoral director" to describe the community building task of the minister.[27] Niebuhr's image has often been criticized as too much a "baptizing" of a management oriented, non- theological view of the ministry appropriate to the post World War II suburban church. This was clearly not what Niebuhr had in mind. He criticized what he calls "the big operator" image of ministry where there is a kind of mindless, uncritical involvement in directing a plethora of activities which have little to do with the *church's* work. Such an image is another way of describing the Managerial model which, as I noted, Alasdair MacIntyre says has come to be a dominant social type today. Instead of MacIntyre's Manager, Niebuhr derived his image from the monastic tradition and intended by it the kind of leadership in community building informed by theological understanding which I am urging as a core leadership task of the clergy professional. Such a role, as Niebuhr notes, has historic links with the role of bishop or *episcopos* who functioned as overseer of a congregation and later of multiple congregations in the early years of the church.

The third area in which the clergy are called on to exercise leadership is what I have called managing the interface between the church and its social context, beginning with the local community. The church, in its congregational expression, is a local institution, and its members are called to participate in the continuing ministry of Jesus in that community. A basic task of the church, therefore, is that of empowering members for this participation. In part, clergy assist in this empowering role through the tasks of meaning definition or interpretation and community building. As church members better understand the relation of their faith to the issues they confront in their daily lives and as they experience the church as a supportive community, they are empowered to act on their faith and understanding in all aspects of life. Or at least, that is how it should work—but here, I believe, something more is required, especially of clergy.

In the previously mentioned research on religion and public life in Hartford, we studied a number of congregations and found among them quite different orientations to public life: some stressing activism on the part of the congregation on social issues, others emphasizing educating members about the issues but leaving any concrete action up to individuals, others placing primary emphasis on converting individuals but not on social issues, and yet others viewing the church primarily as a sanctuary apart from the world with little or no emphasis on either evangelism or social concern.[28] While space prevents further description of the different orientations, what is significant to note here is that we found pastoral leadership to be among the most important factors in determining the dominant orientation in each of the congregations. How pastors defined and interpreted the church's role in public life, including the role of individual members, and how pastors modeled that role in their own involvement in the life of the community were crucial to the congregation's orientation and involvement (or lack of involvement) in public life and that of its members. Additionally, we found that, among community leaders, religion was heavily identified with religious professionals. Unless ministers, priests, or rabbis were themselves visible in public affairs, religion itself was often viewed as absent. There are clearly problems with such a view from a perspective of shared ministry. It is laity and not clergy who are daily inhabitants of the institutions of the public world and whose primary calling is to exercise their ministries in them; nevertheless, the study revealed a need for clergy expertise at this church-social context interface. The expertise includes not only recognizing and playing the important symbolic role expected of clergy as institutional representatives of religion in public life, but also the capacity to analyze community dynamics and public issues, understand them in relation to the Christian tradition, and engage with others (within and outside the church) in ethical reflection on the issues. There are times too when skills in community organization are needed. Many clergy, whose theological education in recent years has included a heavy orientation to counseling with individuals and issues of personal growth, are often ill- prepared for functioning at this interface.

In these three broad areas the church needs the kind of competent clergy leadership implied in the professional model; but, as I have taken pains to emphasize, it is leadership that is able to function interdependently with laity, acknowledging, affirming and supporting their gifts and calling them to ministry. A reconceptualization of the professional model along these lines has, I believe, the potential of avoiding the kind of clericalism, set-apartness, and lay dependency that critics of the model have decried.

Before leaving the subject of clergy-lay relations, however, let me enter a brief caveat against the tendency I perceive in some to romanticism about mutuality between clergy and laity that ignores the positive functions of peer identification among clergy professionals (which the professional model stresses) and the dysfunctions of too heavy an identification with congregational members. I strongly believe in the shared ministry of laity and clergy; however, in the less-than-perfect world of the church—especially in churches with strongly congregational polities—I believe it essential to acknowledge that laicism can be as demonic as clericalism and professionalism. In such situations, clergy can come to be treated as employees of the congregation rather than as ones called to speak with authority a "word from the Lord" when that word is as disturbing one. As a counterbalance to congregational control, being identified with professional peers provides an alternative form of social control and support in clergy functioning. The importance of this alternative to lay control is illustrated in the study of the role of clergy in the Little Rock school desegregation conflict of the 1950s. Sociologists Ernest Campbell and Thomas Pettigrew found that clergy who took a stand supporting school desegregation were much more likely to have what they called a "professional reference system" than a "member reference system." That is, they were much more likely to identify with their denomination and find support from other clergy professionals than to identify primarily with the lay members of their congregations. Laity provided little support for prophetic ministry, while clergy peers and denominational officials were more likely to be supportive.[29] Many of us can attest from personal experience to similar discoveries of the importance of peer and denominational support.

There are no clergy associations that have the same degree of formal social control that bar or medical associations have for lawyers or physicians because of their role in licensing. The nearest formal equivalent to such associations for clergy is the denomination, which in most polities provides some degree of extra-congregational social control and support to clergy in contrast to lay control. Informal or unofficial peer relationships with other clergy are also quite important in providing a degree of social control and support, if not leverage, which supplements that provided more formally at the denominational level. Such relationships at best do not set clergy off against laity, but provide instead the necessary professional distance that enables clergy to function more faithfully and effectively in their congregations.

(2) The Reflective Practice of Ministry

Let me come back to the issue of clergy competence and focus now on the particular issue raised by the second critique of the professional model of ministry. For all of its liabilities, one of the greatest strengths of the model is its emphasis on competence or expertise which, as I noted at the outset, is a primary basis for granting authority to professionals. Although various attributes of clergy are highly valued, few congregations that I know would say that competent clergy leadership, such as that implied in the professional model of ministry, is unimportant. Yet, as will be recalled, the second criticism had to do with the tendency of proponents of the model to foster a kind of instrumental, technically rational approach to ministry devoid of theological vision. As I attempted to point out in the discussion of each of the three general areas of clergy functioning, there is a need to avoid this kind of approach to ministry.

But what more specifically does this imply? Let me try to say more about how this second liability of the professional model of ministry can be avoided. Beyond, or more appropriately beneath, the particular competencies needed for the various roles of ministry that I have considered, I believe that expertise in theological reflection and envisioning is essential. It is the capacity to engage in the practice of ministry out of a clearly articulated vision of the task of the church which gives coherence and direction to the practice. To emphasize this as the fundamental competence needed in no way downplays the need for theological knowledge or for particular skills for ministry; however, it implies that the knowledge and skills be grounded and integrated in a vision of the church and its ministry. The lack of such a vision, I believe, is at the root of the relatively uncritical, mechanical application of various theories and techniques of ministerial practice that critics have said the professional model encourages. But what more specifically does this imply?

As I struggled with this question, I discovered a recent book by Donald Schoen, a social scientist who teaches urban planning at the Massachusetts Institution of Technology. Titled *The Reflective Practitioner. How Professionals Think in Action*, Schoen's book is based on his work as a consultant to various professionals and his observation of their work.[30] He begins his discussion by noting the growing number of leaders in the various professions who write or speak of a crisis of confidence about their profession. Their concern stems from what they perceive as a "mismatch of traditional patterns of practice and knowledge to features of the practice situation—complexity, uncertainty, uniqueness, and value conflict. . . ."

However, instead of despairing over these failures of traditional patterns of professional practice and expertise, Schoen proposes a different understanding of professional expertise, or better, a different method of professional practice.

Schoen's discussion of this alternative understanding of professional practice is derived from observation and analysis of the ways that competent practitioners from several different professions confront difficult situations of practice, situations for which there are no ready made answers or standard repertoire of techniques that can be applied in a relatively unreflective manner. From his observation and analysis, he found a somewhat similar pattern or method of professional practice across the professions when practitioners confronted complex, unusual situations. The pattern, which he calls "reflective conversation with the situation," includes the following elements which are brought variously into play by reflective professionals:

- Skills in analyzing a situation one is confronting in an effort to frame the problem and understand what the issues are.

- Values or "appreciative systems" which also aid in framing the problem and evaluating and reflecting on the situation as one proceeds.

- Overarching theories which supply language and themes for making sense of phenomena in the situation.

- An understanding of the professional's own role in the situation, both its limits and its opportunities.

- The ability to listen to what Schoen calls "talkback" from the situation as one acts in it, learning from the situation and adjusting one's practice in light of this "talkback."

- Willingness to treat one's clients—or in the clergy's case, one's parishioners—as "reflective practitioners" as well with knowledge, insights and abilities which contribute to the solution of the problem at hand.

Schoen's discussion of these elements and their variations from profession to profession is much more complex and subtle than this brief summary of them indicates.[32] Suffice it to say that this model of reflective practice provides, I believe, a way of addressing constructively the second criticism of the professional model that I noted.

Let me attempt to translate the pattern observed by Schoen into terms relevant to the practice of ministry.

- The needed competence includes the capacity to act in ministry situations in terms of the minister's ultimate commitments which direct attention to particular goals or ends as desirable.

- At the same time, the minister will be able to draw on relevant theory and methods, theological and nontheological: examples from the history of the church as it has acted in similar situations in the past; perspectives from theology and ethics which provide interpretations of the good and of human nature and society; and, where relevant, perspectives from philosophy, the arts, and the social sciences which provide additional insights and tools for understanding and action in the situation.

- The reflective practitioner will also be able to analyze the ministry context, its opportunities and constraints.

- Additionally, he or she will bring a characteristic way of framing his or her (and the church's) role in such situations.

- Finally, he or she will treat others in the situations, not as dependent clients, but reflective practitioners who bring their own insights and gifts to the situation.

No one of these elements of reflective practice will of itself provide answers as to how the minister should act in the situation; but out of the dynamic interaction of the various elements, as the minister listens to what Schoen calls "talk-back" from the situation, his or her response will be shaped. While both clergy and laity need to be "reflective practitioners" along these lines, I believe that such competence is especially required of clergy professionals as they function as "first among equals" in exercising leadership in the church's ministry.[33]

The competence of reflective practice, I believe, is not simply one more skill for ministry that is needed alongside others. Rather, as I said previously, I believe that it is a necessary method for the exercise of more specific skills in each of the three broad areas of clergy functioning: meaning defining, community building, and managing the interface between the church and the community. Or, to be more specific, reflective practice is called for in liturgical leadership, preaching, teaching, counseling, program development, parish administration, planning, problem solving, conflict management, community ministry and other roles of ordained clergy. Unless these roles are practiced reflectively, they risk being applied mechanically in the technically rational, managerial style criticized above and illustrated in the second of the three scenarios.

Recalling too the emphasis on shared ministry, let me add my conviction that the professional minister who functions as reflective practitioner in these various roles of ministry will do so, not as the expert who "knows best," or the "Herr Pastor" whose word is "gospel." Rather, in his or her various roles, the minister will function as one with particular insights and skills, based on specialized training, that complement and supplement the insight and skills brought to the situation by lay members who, themselves, are encouraged to be reflective practitioners. Laity will thus be empowered to exercise their ministries as reflective Christians both in the gathered life of the church and in the world. As Schoen describes it more generally, the reflective professional gives up "the rewards of unquestioned authority," the "comfort of relative invulnerability" and the "gratifications of deference" sometimes associated with the traditional professional model. "The new satisfactions open to him [or her] are largely those of discovery—about the meanings of his advice to clients [parishioners], about his knowledge-in-practice, and about himself."[34] And I would add: the rewards of mutuality with laity who bring their gifts of ministry to the life and tasks of the church.

(3) Calling, Spirituality and the Profession of Ministry

So far, in my suggestions for rethinking the professional model of ministry, I seem to be placing most of the emphasis on what a minister *does*—on the expertise in reflective practice which she or he brings to the ministry situation—and neglecting the *being* of the minister, her or his spiritual depth, insight and authenticity. The neglect of being in favor of doing, it will be recalled, was the third criticism of the professional model of ministry. Let me turn finally to this issue and try to see it in relation to the other dimensions of the reconceived professional model of ministry. Again, if I focus here primarily on the being of the ordained minister, it is not because I do not believe that a similar concern also needs to be addressed to lay ministry, but because my concern here is primarily with clergy.

In my review of the criticisms of the professional model of ministry, I suggested that the concern for the spirituality of the clergy is closely related to that of the minister's calling, the former expressing a more Catholic way of stating the issue, the latter more Protestant. Some may object to combining the two emphases. They may argue that the doctrine of calling has to do with more than the minister's spirituality and includes, as well, her or his gifts for ministry and the church's recognition of the appropriateness of those gifts for ordained ministry—what has been called the "ecclesiastical call." I acknowledge this to be the case, but I still believe that it is not incorrect to see a close relationship between the concern for a called ministry, particularly in Gilbert Tennent's plea for a converted ministry, and a concern for ministry that is spiritually authentic. And it is on the relationship of these two issues that I want to focus this section, especially because of the criticism that the professional model of ministry ignores these dimensions in favor of emphasis on expertise.

I called attention in the Introduction to two penultimate bases of a clergyperson's authority: that based on knowledge and expertise and that based on her or his relationship to God. In a conceptual sense, it is probably helpful to distinguish between these two bases of authority, the former having to do particularly with professional authority and the latter having to do more with charismatic or sacred authority. One gains the former especially through an educational process; the latter comes from an encounter with the Holy, whether in a dramatic sense of call like that of Isaiah or a sense of vocation developed over a period of time through a process of spiritual formation. The two kinds of authority derive from different sources and are different. For the sake of conceptual clarity, it seems to make sense to distinguish them. But distinctions that are useful conceptually are neither necessary nor helpful when it comes to the reality of the person and functioning of the minister.

To be sure, such separation sometimes occurs not just conceptually but actually. And I am not referring only to those whose frenzied preaching generates much emotional heat without shedding much light. That does happen, and one need only listen to some of the radio preachers to recognize the phenomenon. But I refer especially to clergy whose spirituality is of a "quieter" sort, clergy who are respected for their genuine piety but lack the basic competence needed to function effectively in the various roles of ministry. A layperson once commented to me about her pastor that if she had a serious problem, she would not think of going to him for help. "He is so good that he wouldn't understand." She meant that (I think) as a compliment, but in fact she damned him with not-so- faint praise. Unfortunately, she was mostly correct in her assessment. His was a kind of piety that made it difficult for him to understand many of the issues that confronted his parishioners in the way that reflective practice necessitates.

And it is equally true that one can have expertise without the authenticity that comes from calling as the third scenario illustrated. In an article in *Theology Today*, Thomas Long makes this point graphically. Moses and Aaron, paired as leaders of Israel, reflect together the combination of the two bases of authority I have been describing: Moses with his profound relationship to the mystery that is God; Aaron without the vision but with the gifts of public speaking which Moses lacked. Their gifts are complementary, and all goes well so long as they hold them together. But, while Moses, the "Vision," was on the mountaintop, Aaron, the "Expertise" was in the valley, under pressure from the people to point God out. As Long puts it vividly:

> Finally Aaron yields and does what ministerial practice always does when it is cut off from its vision of the active presence of God; he fashions a god for them from the materials at hand. Since there is no Mystery, there is only mechanical method. Pastoral care becomes the realization of human potential. Preaching becomes "possibility thinking." Administration becomes institutional maintenance. The sacraments become audio-visual aids, and worship has only a "near horizon." The Christian life becomes the sad and wearing business of rolling out the golden calf forged out of our best intentions and pleading with it to make us whole.[35]

The importance of holding together calling and expertise receives added emphasis in a suggestive exploratory study by John Fletcher. Laity were asked by Fletcher to describe factors affecting their relationships with clergy. The clergy attribute most often mentioned as enabling laity to establish deeply personal relationships with clergy is what Fletcher labeled "religious authenticity." It was described variously by laity as having "head and heart together," as being reflected in the clergyperson who "lives the gospel," or who is both "a man of God and a man of the world." While Fletcher found that expertise was highly valued by the laity, that which authenticated the clergy to them and made possible the establishment of deep personal bonds was religious authenticity. It is a minister's personal or religious authenticity and integrity that not only enhances the relationship of clergy and laity, but such authenticity and integrity are essential if laity are to trust the clergy's expertise and leadership as a professional.[36]

Let me add that the need for the combination of expertise combined with integrity is not restricted to the profession of ministry. It is a mistake to think that being professional and having a calling are mutually exclusive, as some critics of the professional model have implied. Recall that the various attributes of a profession that I cited previously (see page 4), included not only the professional's special knowledge and expertise, but also his or her "calling." What Wilbert Moore means by calling here is "an enduring set of normative and behavioral expectations," having to do especially with persistence in one's profession, commitment to its norms and standards, and loyalty to one's peers.[37] Calling also includes the professional's integrity, trustworthiness and commitment to service. Understanding one's profession as a calling includes an expectation that one will use her or his expertise responsibly for the good of the community.

To be sure, a profession's emphasis on calling can be just so much rhetoric: it can be and has been used ideologically by professors to justify the profession's claims to special privileges and high status. Yet, there are important positive reasons for maintaining the emphasis on calling in the professions generally. In an analysis of the role of trust in society, sociologist Bernard Barber points out that one does not trust a professional—grant her or him authority over some important aspect of one's life—only on the basis of a belief that the professional has the necessary expertise in the situation. There is also an expectation of fiduciary responsibility on the part of the professional. "Technically competent performance can be monitored insofar as it is based on shared knowledge and expertise. But when some parties to a social relationship or some members of a social system cannot comprehend that expertise, performance can be controlled by trust. A fiduciary obligation is placed on the holder and user of the special knowledge and skills with regard to the other members of his social system."[38] James Gustafson has put it more forcefully in an article on calling in the professions:

> A "calling" without professionalization is bumbling, ineffective, and even dangerous. A profession without a calling, however, has no taps of moral and human rootage to keep motivation alive, to keep human sensitivities and sensibilities alert, and to nourish a proper sense of self-fulfillment. Nor does a profession without a calling easily envision the larger ends and purposes of human good that our individual efforts can serve.[39]

Although many nonclergy professionals may not think of their fiduciary responsibility in terms of a call from God, there are "ghosts" of such experiences inhabiting their more secularized version of calling. It is important that this sense of calling be nourished and enlivened for all professions and not simply for ordained ministry. For nonclergy professionals who are Christians, it is important that they be helped to affirm their calling as a part of the ministry in which they share.

But let me come back now to clergy as professionals and simply reiterate, by way of summary, that here especially doing and being, expertise and authenticity, cannot finally be separated as bases of clergy authority without doing great damage to ministry. The importance of religious authenticity in the professional minister's relationships with laity, as well as the need to bring one's deep faith commitments (not only one's knowledge) to bear in one's reflective practice, make it imperative that calling be understood as an essential dimension of the professional model of ministry. "Moses" and "Aaron", spiritual vision and expertise, or what John Wesley called "knowledge and vital piety" must be held together. By holding them together, is it not also possible that clergy will model a union of expertise and authenticity that will help other professionals (and nonprofessional laity as well) to affirm their own sense of calling and fiduciary responsibility in their work?

The implications of all of this for continuing personal and professional growth are many. Let me simply list them as a series of questions without trying to supply the answers.

- What does it mean for us to nourish our relationship to God to keep alive that sense of being called without which our leadership is vacuous and even dangerous?

- What spiritual disciplines are necessary to insure that our reflective practice of ministry is enlivened by a personal sense of the Holy?

- What disciplines are necessary to foster that kind of integrity, authenticity, that make trusting and helping relationships possible?

- How can we grow in our relational capacities, our ability to use ourselves as an important ingredient of our practice of ministry?

- What is needed to keep our spirituality turned outward rather than inward so that it fosters commitment to the continuing struggle for peace and justice?

These are some of the issues that must be addressed in the effort to hold together calling and expertise, knowledge and vital piety, in a reconceived professional model of ministry.

Conclusion

In the Introduction, I raised the question, "Is the professional model of ministry worth saving?" In the course of trying to give an affirmative answer, I have tried to respond to several of the more important criticisms that have been made of the model. It is easy, I believe, to set up the professional model of ministry as a kind of "straw person" and find a number of ways that it is inappropriate for ministry. While some of the critics of the model seem guilty of this, I believe that some of the criticism is merited, and I have tried to take it seriously in suggesting how the model might be reconceived rather than discarded.

To be sure, there are other models of ministry, past and present, available to the church; and there will surely be others in the future. Given the pluralism that exists today as the church tries to be faithful in a variety of different contexts, there are many situations where the professional model may not be the most appropriate one. I would simply acknowledge this while at the same time expressing my conviction regarding its continuing relevance in some contexts, including our own.

I have tried to spell out its relevance in terms of clergy able to function interdependently with lay Christians as they share the ministry of the church. In their commitment to shared ministry these clergy nevertheless recognize the need for a differentiation of functions in both the gathered and scattered life of the church, and they are able to claim their own particular authority in some areas of leadership while respecting and enabling that of the laity in others. I have suggested that, in the exercise of leadership in specific roles of ministry, a fundamental competence needed by clergy professionals is the ability to function as reflective practitioners in a variety of specific roles of ministry. This includes the capacity, in these various roles, to analyze difficult and often novel situations and bring one's beliefs, commitments, knowledge and skills to bear in such a way that one's response is both appropriate to the situation and grounded in a vision of ministry. Such expertise can in part be learned, but *only* in part. For it must also grow out of a sense of calling from which the vision of ministry springs and which also is the ground of the minister's personal authenticity and integrity. It is in the wedding of calling and the competence of reflective practice that I believe lies the hope for vital professional leadership in the shared ministry of the church.

ENDNOTES

1. Celia A. Hahn and James R. Adams (Washington, DC: The Alban Institute, 1980).

2. An earlier version of this paper, focused on theological education, was published as "The Professional Model of Ministry—Is It Worth Saving?," *Theological Education* (XXI, Spring, 1985: 7-48). My research was made possible by a grant from the Association of Theological Schools.

3. Jackson W. Carroll, "Some Issues in Clergy Authority" *Review of Religious Research* 23 (December 1981: 99-117).

4. James Glasse, *Profession Minister* (Nashville: Abingdon, 1968).

5. See especially E. Brooks Holifield, *A History of Pastoral Care in America* (Nashville: Abingdon, 1983).

6. "Theological Education and Models for Ministry", *The St. Luke's Journal of Theology* XXV (March 1982: 158).

7. *The Clerical Profession*, (London: SPCK, 1980).

8. *The Culture of Professionalism*, (New York: W.W. Norton, 1976, p. x).

9. For a history of these turf wars in the field of medicine, see Paul Starr, *The Social Transformation of Modern Medicine*, (New York: Basic Books, 1982).

Donald Scott, *From Office to Profession* (Philadelphia: University of Pennsylvania Press, 1978, pp. 145-155.

11. Cited in Robert W. Lynn, *"Why the Seminary?"*, unpublished manuscript, 1978.

12. Wilbert Moore, *The Professions: Roles and Rules* (New York: Russell Sage, 1970, p. 5).

13. Bernard Cooke, *Ministry to Word and Sacraments* (Philadelphia: Fortress Press, 1976), p. 266.

14. See Jackson W. Carroll and Robert L. Wilson, *Too Many Pastors? The Clergy Job Market* (New York: Pilgrim Press, 1980), pp. 103- 5.

15. Donald Scott, *From Office to Profession*, p. 63

16. Daniel Calhoun, *Professional Lives in America* (Cambridge: Harvard University Press, 1965), p. 171.

17. A particularly insightful discussion of these problems is found in Edward Farley's book, *Theologia* (Philadelphia: Fortress Press, 1983), in which he sharply criticizes the dominance of the professional model of ministry, which he refers to as the "clerical paradigm," in theological education.

18. Alasdair MacIntyre, *After Virtue* (Notre Dame: Notre Dame Press, 1981), pp. 26ff. See also Joseph C. Hough, Jr., "The Education of Practical Theologians" (*Theological Education* XX, Spring, 1984): pp. 77-8.

19. Urban Holmes, *The Priest in Community* (New York: Seabury, 1978), p. 67.

20. In H. Shelton Smith, Robert T. Handy, and Lefferts A. Loetscher, *American Christianity, an Historical Interpretation with Representative Documents* (New York: Charles Scribner's Sons, 1960), p. 326.

21. Robert Baird, *Religion in America* (New York: Harper and Brothers, 1856), p. 279.

22. For readers wishing to pursue the matter further, I would recommend Avery Dulles' *Models of the Church* (Garden City, NY: Doubleday, 1978).

23. For a recent approach to lay ministry in the church that more than adequately complements the position taken here, see Celia Hahn, *Lay Voices in an Open Church* (Washington, DC: Alban Institute, 1985).

24. In an address at the annual meeting of the Society for the Advancement of Continuing Education in Ministry, New York, NY, June 19, 1985. I am also grateful to James Lowery for suggesting the importance of the "wellness" orientation.

25. William J. McKinney, David A. Roozen and Jackson W. Carroll, *Religion's Public Presence* (Washington, DC: The Alban Institute, 1983).

26. James Gustafson, "The Minister as Moral Counselor," unpublished paper, June 20, 1982.

27. H. Richard Niebuhr, *The Purpose of the Church and Its Ministry*, (New York: Harper & Row, 1956), pp. 79ff.

28. See David A. Roozen, William McKinney, and Jackson W. Carroll, *The Varieties of Religious Presence* (New York: The Pilgrim Press, 1984).

29. Ernest Campbell and Thomas Pettigrew, "Racial and Moral Crisis: the Role of Little Rock Ministers," *American Journal of Sociology* 64 (March 1959): 509-16.

30. Donald Schoen, *The Reflective Practitioner, How Professionals Think in Action* (New York: Basic Books, 1983).

31. Ibid., p. 18.

32. For a more extended discussion, see especially Ibid., pp. 267-83.

33. For an extended discussion of a method of ministry similar to that of Schoen's, see James D. Whitehead and Evelyn Eaton Whitehead, *Method in Ministry, Theological Reflection and Christian Ministry,* (New York: Seabury, 1981).

34. Schoen, *The Reflective Practitioner*, p. 299.

35. Thomas Long, "Moses, Aaron, and Practical Theology," *Theology Today*, XLII, April 1985, p. 1.

36. John Fletcher, *Religious Authenticity in the Clergy* (Washington, DC: The Alban Institute, 1975).

37. Wilbert Moore, *The Professions*, pp. 7-9.

38. Bernard Barber, *The Logic and Limits of Trust* (New Brunswick, NJ: Rutgers University Press, 1983. p. 15.

39. James Gustafson, "Professions as 'Callings,'" *The Social Service Review*, 56, December 1982, p. 514.

You may also be interested in these Alban Institute Publications

Religion's Public Presence by William J. McKinney, David A. Roozen, Jackson W. Carroll
Religious presence, its influence and impact in the public life of Hartford, Connecticut, is the focus of this major study by the Center for Social and Religious Research of the Hartford Seminary, and the United Church Board for Homeland Ministries, New York, NY. The study includes interviews with social, business, government, education, and professional leaders. The compilation and analysis of these interviews helped Hartford churches and synagogues to understand their communities, to reflect on what they want to be, and to develop strategies for effective public ministry. A Study Guide and an Interview Guide are included for you to adapt to your own communities. (AL61 $6.25)

Religious Authenticity in the Clergy by John C. Fletcher
The stages of growth between a pastor and congregation are conceptualized in a fresh way. Three crises emerge through which a clergy person becomes authenticated as minister of a congregation. (AL10, $3.75)

Generation to Generation: Family Process in Church and Synagogue by Edwin H. Friedman
The application of family systems theories to the emotional processes at work in: 1) congregational life; 2) in the families of parishioners; and 3) the clergy's own family offers new insights to congregational leaders. Because of their position and entree into congregational families, clergy have opportunities to be a catalyst to change in a way not available to other helping professionals. Analyzing the interlock between the three systems, Rabbi Friedman shows how the way clergy function generally as congregational leaders can have more therapeutic impact on member families than what is said or done in specific counseling sessions. The systemic approach of Leadership Through Self-Differentiation (rather than through charisma or consensus) offers possibilities of increased power and diminished stress. (AL86, $25.00)

Lay Voices in an Open Church by Celia Allison Hahn
"Hahn bases her work on recent research, but its charm comes from the concrete ideas she relates. She combines common sense, theology, observation and patience to come up with formulas that will help people understand their lives and functions as laity." *The Christian Century*

"She makes a clear distinction between the Closed Church and the

Open Church, the Church as a World in Itself and the Church in the World, and shows why the Open Church does a better job of equipping the laity for their ministries. Who should read this useful little book? Certainly anyone who cares about the church and the frustrating gap between the vision and the reality of its potential. Certainly anyone with responsibilities in the church—vestries, clergy, councils, lay leaders." *Cathedral Age* (AL83, $7.25)

Stress, Power and Ministry by John C. Harris
A "classic" Alban Institute publication, this handbook for clergy and laity is a result of many years of sensitive work with many churches. Mr. Harris explores the extraordinarily complex, tender, creative, and frightening relationships between the work of clergy and the life of laity. (AL27, $8.25. Study Guide, AL27SG, $2.75)

The Whole Church Catalog edited by Dr. James F. Hopewell and developed by the Project Team for Congregational Studies
This guide will help you find 131 instruments that churches and their consultants use to understand and alter the corporate behavior of congregations. This major reference book is particularly helpful to pastors, executives, consultants, trainers, researchers, D.Min. candidates, seminary practical theology and field education departments, and continuing education programs. Two indexes and a useful grid help the reader locate the right design for the purpose intended and indicate how to get the design. (AL79, $21.00, three-ring binder included)

Explorations in Faith, Leaders' Guide by Robert A. Evans, G. Douglass Lewis, Marjorie Hall Davis
Presented in the context of real-life issues that puzzle and trouble us all, this six-session course developed at the Hartford Seminary enables clergy and laity to share theological resources. Session titles are: "What is Faith?"; "Meaning"; "Belonging"; "Empowering"; "Acting in the World"; and "Facing Death". Two educational methods are highlighted: Bible study with detailed instruction by Walter Wink; and case studies to provide a real-life context for the issues. Six 2 1/2 hour sessions are carefully outlined. (Leader's Guide AL58, $8.75; Participants' Packet AL58P, $3.75)

$1.50 handling charge on each order. Orders under $25 must be prepaid. No postage charged on prepaid orders.